W9-BBZ-746

Amazing World of Spiders

Written by Janet Craig

Illustrated by Jean Helmer

Troll Associates

Library of Congress Cataloging-in-Publication Data

Amazing world of spiders.

Summary: Discusses the characteristics and behavior
of different kinds of spiders.
    1. Spiders—Juvenile literature.   [1. Spiders]
I. Helmer, Jean Cassels, ill.   II. Title.
QL458.4.P35   1990   595.4´4   89-5005
ISBN 0-8167-1751-6 (lib. bdg.)
ISBN 0-8167-1752-4 (pbk.)

Copyright © 1990 by Troll Associates

All rights reserved. No part of this book may be used or
reproduced in any manner whatsoever without written
permission from the publisher.
Printed in the United States of America.
10   9

They live in trees or on the ground. You'll find them on the highest mountain or deep in a cave, in a shady swamp or a dry, hot desert. Some even live under water. Now look in your house—chances are they live there, too!

Can you guess what they are? They are spiders, and they will live anywhere they can find food. There are almost thirty thousand kinds of spiders. And scientists think there are thousands more yet to be discovered.

Spiders come in many sizes. Some, like the comb-footed spider, are no bigger than a speck of dust. Others are as large as a person's hand. The biggest spider of all is the hairy-looking tarantula of South America. With its legs stretched out, this giant measures ten inches (25 centimeters) long.

You may think a spider is an insect, like a bee or an ant. Although a spider looks a bit like an insect, it is not an insect. Spiders are part of a group of animals called *arachnids*. Some other arachnids are ticks, mites, and scorpions.

If a spider and an insect were placed side by side, you could clearly see differences between the two.

One of the biggest differences is the number of legs each has. A spider has eight legs, while an insect has six.

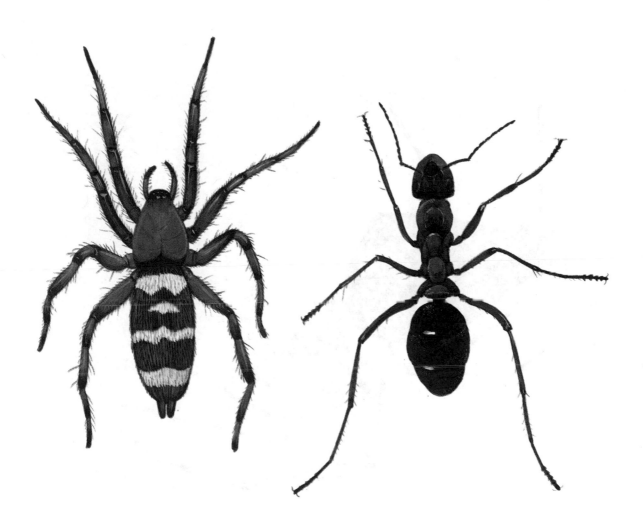

Another difference is the shape of their bodies. A spider's body has two main parts, joined by a tiny waist. These are the back part, called the *abdomen,* and the front part, called the *cephalothorax.* This word means "head-chest"—and that is exactly what it is.

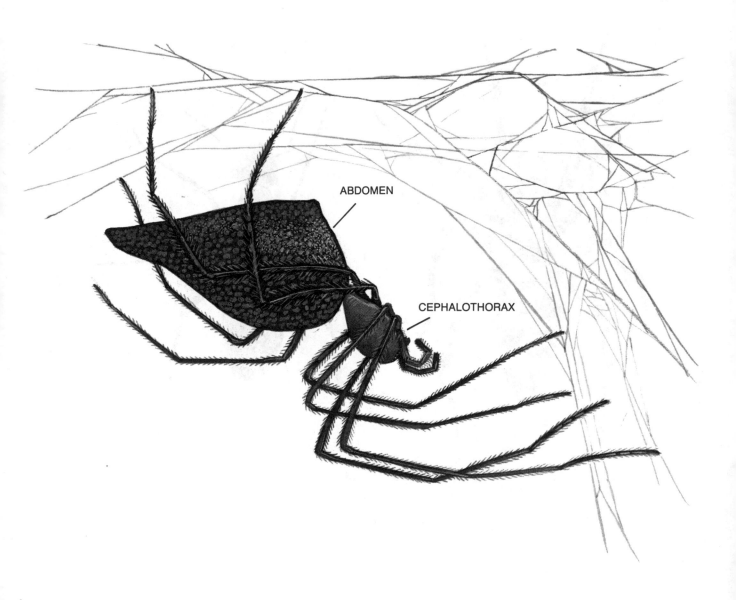

ABDOMEN

CEPHALOTHORAX

ANTENNAE

HEAD

THORAX

ABDOMEN

An insect has three main body parts: a head, a thorax (the middle part), and an abdomen.

Insects also have feelers called *antennae* on their heads, which spiders do not have. And unlike spiders, many insects have wings.

A spider does not have a backbone like a dog or a horse or a person. Instead the spider's body is covered by a tough skin. This thin, but strong, skin protects the spider's inner parts.

The skin and legs of the spider are covered by tiny hairs. These hairs help the spider's sense of touch—they are excellent feelers.

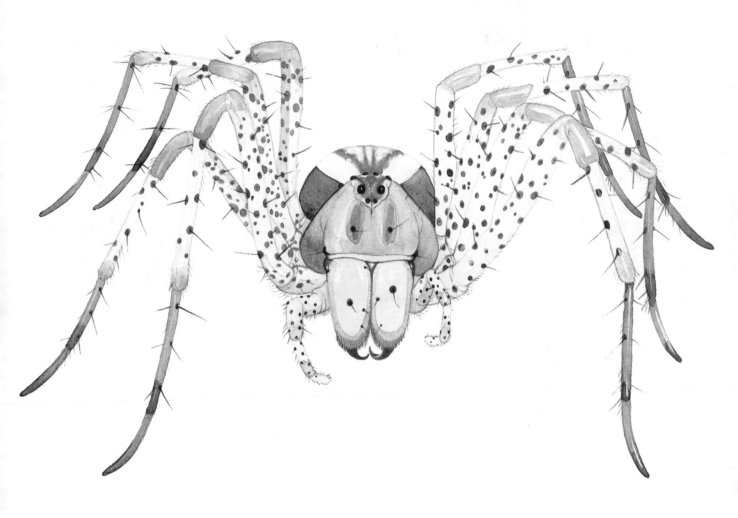

    Most spiders have eight eyes, placed in two rows across their heads. But even with so many eyes, most spiders cannot see very well or very far.

    Nature has made up for the spider's poor eyesight by giving it a very special ability—that is its ability to spin silk. Silk helps the spider do many jobs. One of the most important ways spiders use silk is to spin webs in which to catch food.

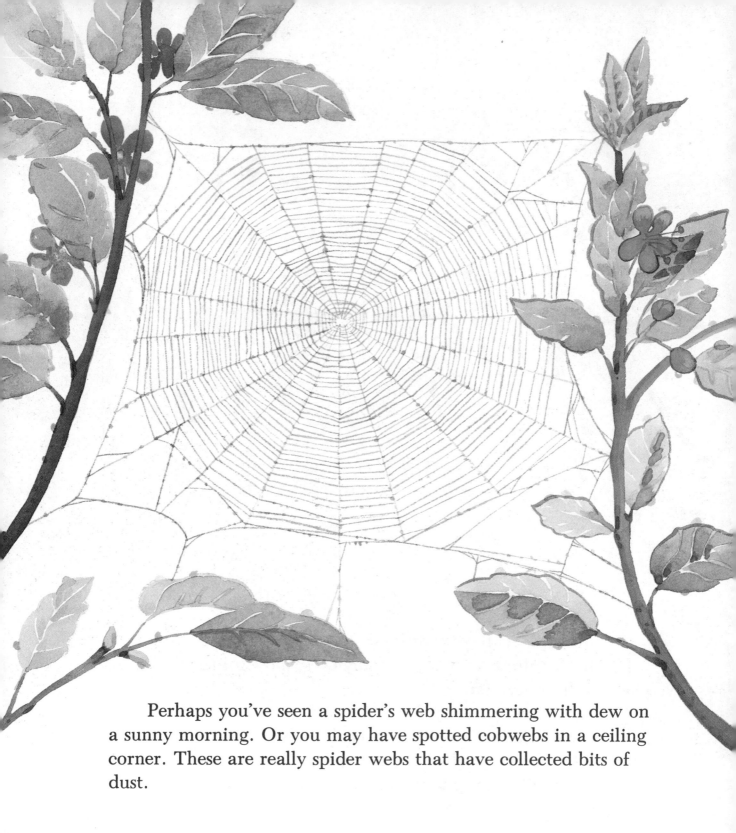

Perhaps you've seen a spider's web shimmering with dew on a sunny morning. Or you may have spotted cobwebs in a ceiling corner. These are really spider webs that have collected bits of dust.

How does a spider make silk for its web? At the end of the spider's abdomen are special parts called *spinnerets*. These are like tiny tubes or faucets from which the silk comes. When it first comes out, the silk is liquid. As the air hits it, the silk hardens into thread.

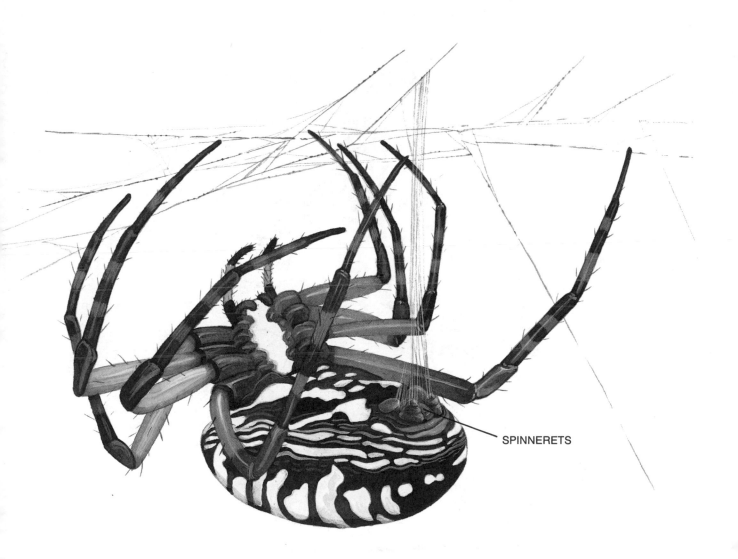

SPINNERETS

Scientists have counted seven types of spinnerets. But not all spiders have all seven spinnerets. All spiders have at least three spinnerets, and most have six.

Each spinneret makes a different kind of silk. Some silk is sticky, some is not. Some threads are thin, some are thicker. Spider silk is very strong. In fact, a line of spider silk is stronger than steel wire of the same size.

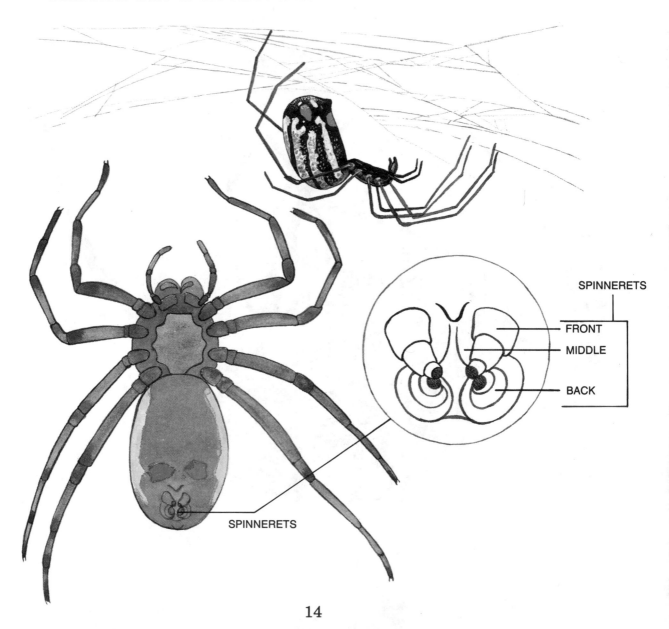

SPINNERETS

SPINNERETS

FRONT

MIDDLE

BACK

   Everywhere a spider goes, it spins a special thread behind it called a *dragline*. The spider's safety depends upon its dragline. If an enemy comes near the web, a spider can drop quickly down the dragline to escape.

The pretty orange garden spider weaves a beautiful
rounded web. When an unlucky insect gets tangled in the sticky
web, the spider rushes out and grabs its meal. The spider then
turns the insect around, wrapping it in silk until it cannot move.

Even certain spiders that don't spin webs use silk to capture food. The bolas spider uses silk thread the way a cowboy uses a lasso. The spider spins a single strand of silk with a sticky drop at the end of it. The spider waits. When an insect flies near, the spider swings the thread. If the spider's aim is good, the insect will stick to the line.

Spiders have another use for their silk. They spin sturdy, waterproof silk sacs, or bags, in which they lay their eggs.

Scientists often divide spiders into two groups, depending on the way they catch their food. These groups are the web-spinning spiders and the hunters.

There are many kinds of spider webs, and each is as unique, or special, as the spider that spins it.

HUNTER

Common house spiders spin a *tangled web*. It is a jumble of threads. Such a web is usually attached to the corners of a wall or ceiling.

The tangled web may be shapeless, but it makes a very good trap. When an insect flies into the web, it cannot break free of the sticky silk. The spider rushes out of its hiding place and begins to tie up its victim with silk. If the insect struggles, the spider bites it with its two poison fangs. The bite does not kill the victim, for spiders like to eat only live things. Instead the poison stuns the insect. If the spider is hungry, it will suck the juice out of the unlucky insect. If it is not hungry, the spider saves the meal for later.

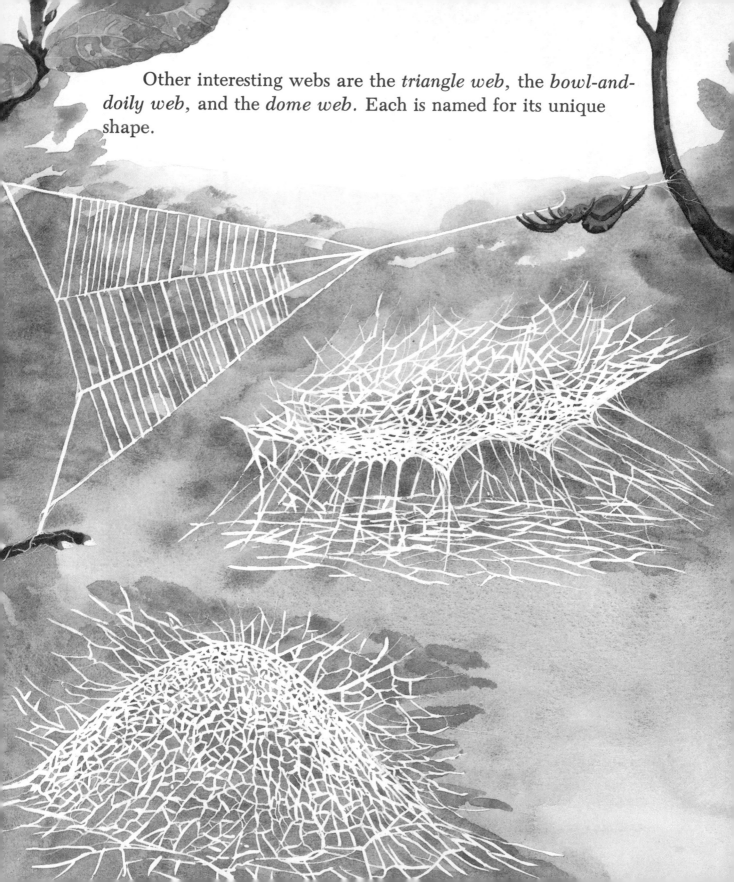

Other interesting webs are the *triangle web*, the *bowl-and-doily web*, and the *dome web*. Each is named for its unique shape.

The *orb web* is the most beautiful of all. This large, round web makes a lovely, delicate design hanging between two branches.

The orb-weaving spider is a talented builder. It begins by spinning a few lines of silk to hold the web up. Next it adds lines of dry silk that look like the spokes of a wheel. At last, it adds a sticky coil around the "spokes." Some orb weavers spin a zigzag band of silk in the middle of the web, where they wait for their prey. Others hide nearby, attached to the web by a trap line.

Why doesn't a spider stick to its own web? There are two reasons. First, the spider's body is covered by oil, which will not stick to silk. Second, the spider knows its own web very well. It runs mostly along the dry silk threads, trying not to touch the sticky ones.

Not all spiders spin webs. The second group of spiders is the hunters, which run after their prey. Tarantulas, wolf spiders, and water spiders are all excellent hunters.

Instead of a web, the tarantula digs a burrow, or hole, in which to live. At night, this strong spider hunts for insects, small snakes, or lizards. The tarantulas that live in the United States are not poisonous to people, although their bite may hurt. Some people even like to raise tarantulas, for they can be very gentle pets.

Wolf spiders live in burrows or beneath rocks. They run quickly after their prey. They are named after wolves because of their swiftness and fine hunting ability.

The water spider is fascinating. It is the only spider that spends nearly all its life underwater.

This special spider spins a bell-shaped web under the water. Next the spider brings tiny air bubbles into the water-proof web. The bubbles push the water out of the web. Now the spider is ready to move into its home. It can stay under water for several months, breathing the air from the bubbles in its web. This spider hunts for water insects, which it brings into its web.

The trapdoor spider digs a tunnel and lines it with silk. For protection, the spider makes a hinged trapdoor from silk and dirt to cover the tunnel. If the spider is hungry, it opens the door just a crack. If an insect passes by, the spider jumps out to catch it.

Crab spiders also ambush their prey. These spiders, which move sideways, as crabs do, wait inside flowers for insects to eat. Crab spiders can change color—from white to yellow—in order to blend in with the flower on which they are hiding.

Spiders, both web spinners and hunters, are good at catching insects. But one insect—the spider wasp—is the spider's worst enemy. The wasp stings the spider, so it cannot move. Then the wasp uses the spider as food for its babies.

Most spiders live for one year, or for a few years, at most. Tarantulas are the exception. Some can live more than twenty years.

When a male spider looks for a mate, he must do so carefully. This is because the female, if hungry, may eat her suitor. Some males wave their bodies and legs in a sort of dance to attract a mate. One spider brings the female an insect to eat. If she accepts this "present," they will become mates.

The mother spider lays her eggs and puts them in a strong silk sac.

The wolf spider carries the egg sac with her. When the babies, called *spiderlings*, hatch, the mother lets them ride on her back.

But most spider mothers do not stay with their babies. When the spiderlings come out of their nest, they lift their backs toward the breeze. The air pulls a small strand of silk from the baby's body. Off the spiderlings float into the air, like tiny balloons on strings. In fact, this way of traveling is called *ballooning*. The breeze can carry the babies great distances to their new homes.

As a baby spider grows, it molts. This means the spider loses its hard, outer covering, which no longer fits. The spider grows, then quickly forms a new skin. If a young spider loses a leg, it can grow a new one when it molts. This is something a fully grown spider cannot do.

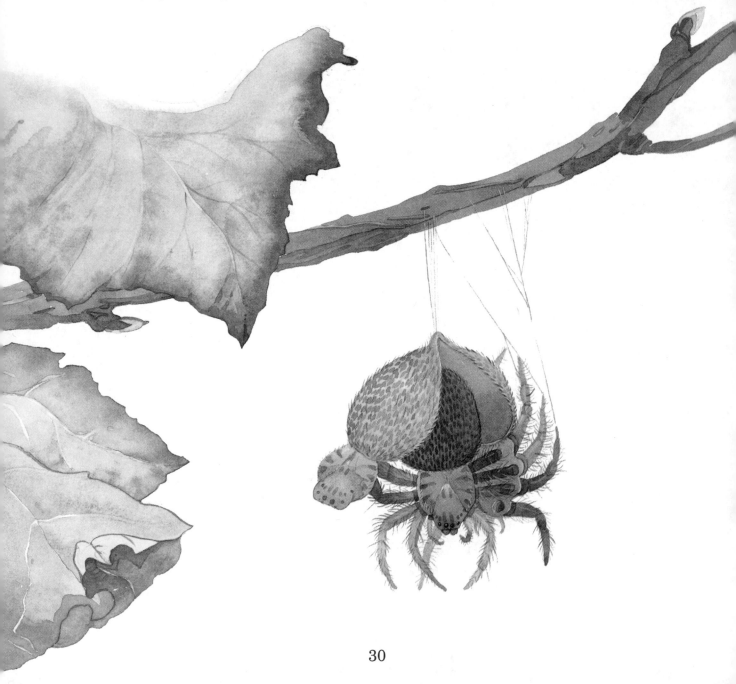

Some people are afraid of spiders. But these animals are really helpful to us because they eat many harmful insects. One of the few spiders that has a bite that is very poisonous to people is the black widow. This spider is shiny black. On its underside is a red or yellow mark that looks a little like an hourglass. If you should see a shiny black spider, be sure to stay away from it!

But most spiders are very valuable to us. They can be interesting to watch, too. Look for these unusual animals in the grass, in a garden, in flowers, or in your home. You may discover many interesting things about these creatures. Spiders are a special part of the world of nature—a world filled with many wonders.

Index